Red

Flags

How to know he's playing games with you

How to spot a guy who's never going to commit. How to force him to show his cards.

What you will learn in this book:

The author of this book does not dispense medical advice or prescribe the use of any technique as a form of treatment for physical, emotional or medical problems without the advice of a qualified physician, either directly or indirectly. The intent of the author is only to offer information of a general nature to help you in your quest for emotional and spiritual well-being. In the event you use any of the information in this book, the author and the publisher assume no responsibility for your actions.

I Write This Book For You

I wrote this book because I respect you, a woman, more than you will ever know. I've been coaching women since 2008, and it hurts me when I see how my clients create self-fulfilling prophecies. Every one of them deserves a good-looking guy who treats them well. Usually, these women can get him, but they often mess up simply because they don't understand men.

Some of the examples I provide in this book are very poignant. Some may offend you; others might even upset you. You may even think I'm childish or immature for my suggestions and advice. I can assure you, however, I'm not. I'm a man; I know how men think, and I want to uncover my gender's crazy reactions to what women do and don't do.

If you're willing to change some of your dating strategies and transform your thinking, you'll be surprised of what's possible. The man you want will be kissing your feet in no time, or you'll be able to decide he's just not worth it and find someone better.

The red line in this book will be that you shouldn't adapt; you shouldn't change who you are; you shouldn't try to please. You should, instead, know what you're worth, know what you deserve, and be willing to walk away when the guy in your life doesn't measure up. That alone will make you a lot more attractive, and it's only the tip of the iceberg.

But first, ask yourself. On a scale from 1 to 10, what's the level of importance you gave yourself in your last relationships with men? What's the level of importance you gave him?

Please, really take a minute to think about this before you continue.

You'll see that you'll get in trouble with men the minute you make him more important than yourself. Men have built-in radars for this. They all want a woman who's got her stuff together, who has the confidence to know what she's worth. They want someone who knows her attention, her love, needs to be earned. Men want to earn it, chase her, work hard to get her and then, very importantly, work hard to keep her.

Will you allow him to do this?

If you are, that's wonderful. Women who go in the opposite direction often fall into the traps of so-called Game Players.

In what follows you'll learn who they are, why they play games and what you can do about it.

Good luck!
Brian

If You Want a Happy and Healthy Love Life

I'm sure at least one man broke your heart, leaving you without a real explanation or reason as to why. He probably told you it wasn't your fault, but his own. He might have added, "You'll make a man really happy some day." But apparently that man just isn't him.

This can be really frustrating, especially if you've followed all the "rules." You took it slow; you didn't push him, and you were careful not to get hurt. And yet it happened. You still ended up with a broken heart.

Although it truly might be because of something you did, some men lie about what they really feel for you and what their real plans are. They can break up with you at any given time, going from hot to cold in an instant. Those men will take you on an emotional rollercoaster ride and will make your love life a living hell.

In this book, you'll learn what types of men play games, why they play those games, red flags to watch out for, and how to filter the true bad boys out of your life. You'll learn how you can protect your heart from men who don't even deserve your attention, let alone your love and devotion.

I want you to understand what types of men play these games because this will help you identify them a lot sooner. Then I'll teach you some strategies to quickly test him and turn things around. If he doesn't respond well to those tests, at least you can be sure that he's playing with you and it's time to move on.

I've been coaching women for many years now, and it frustrates me when I see how many men simply don't respect women. They play with their hearts, their feelings, and their future. Since I'm a man myself, I know why men do what they do. I'm here to help great women like you who keep walking into the traps of the same disrespectful men.

Men who play games do it with every woman they meet. If you've ever encountered one, it wasn't personal; it's just the way they are built. They don't know any better.

In my series of books, I try to uncover the truth about the man behind the game, so you'll know what's really going on in his mind. In this book, we'll focus on the type of men who play games with women. These men know how to touch a woman's hot buttons, how to make her happy, how to attract her into his trap. The problem is, because they're not genuine, your gut feeling will start to notice the discrepancies, the little white lies, when his words don't align with his actions. That's when the emotional rollercoaster ride starts.

Men who play games, and as you'll see it's not only the player type who does this, know how to hang a carrot on a stick in front of a woman. You might think this only happens to not-so-intelligent women. It doesn't. Some of my clients have very high positions in international companies, household names, lawyers, surgeons, and so on. Yet they too fall for his games and step into his traps.

Some of these men are smart. They are master conmen, master manipulators. Not all of them have bad intentions, as you'll learn; some simply don't know any better. They don't have the emotional intelligence that's needed to reveal their true selves. You'll learn how to spot those men as well.

This makes me think about Sarah, one of my high-end clients; she's a very intelligent and attractive woman in her mid-thirties who is financially secure and has a great job. She's very successful professionally, but in her love life, she keeps falling for the games some men play. And one way or another, she keeps attracting the bad kind. Her problem is that she has a true entrepreneurial mindset, and she also deploys in her love life. She loves a challenge and falls for men who make it hard on her—true Players who give her a mix of hot and cold signals. She fell for the good-looking guys who wouldn't throw themselves at her feet (like all the nice guys she quickly got bored of). When she started a relationship with any of those players, she always thought she could eventually tame them, change them, and turn them into the perfect husband with whom she could start a family.

She was wrong.

As you'll learn later in this book, the real player cannot be changed. It is a waste of time and love to even try. It's important to learn and spot men whom you have no future with early on, so you don't get too invested.

I wonder what you are like when it comes to men. Do you fall for guys who are hard to get? Do you like a challenge? Most women do. Most women don't fall for the typical nice guy who wears his heart on his sleeve. Mind you, even those nice guys can play games by the way, as you'll learn later on in this book.

The Game in the Relationship World

A game is anything that conceals the true meaning of the actions or the final outcome the man wants. Men who play games are not honest. They wear a mask and have ulterior motives. They hide their true plans and intentions, because they know you wouldn't stick around should they reveal them. You should avoid those types of men because it's impossible to have a healthy and secure relationship with them.

Some examples of their games are:

- Telling you he loves you when he knows he doesn't
- Telling you you're the one, while he has others on the side
- Talking about your future together, when he knows he's waiting for someone better
- Running away when you come too close, coming closer when you take a step back

The clearest game that's often played is a guy who tells you exactly what you need to hear, until he can really "have" you and be with you sexually. That was his primary and only goal. Once he gets it, he's gone.

Other games are way more complex, where the man keeps wearing a mask and might actually be in a long-term relationship with you. There's this TV show called "Who on Earth Did I Marry?" on Discovery Investigation. On this show, women find out their husband was a major drug dealer, a criminal, and more. They had no idea since he was playing perfect daddy and husband at home.

Here's one more example of how far a man's games can go. When I was growing up, my parents had good friends with kids the same age as my sister and I. So our get-togethers were really perfect. The parents could have fun, while the kids were having fun as well. We went on long holidays together and had a lot of great experiences.

When I was about twenty, the friends of my parents broke up. The now ex-wife was devastated. Something bad had happened, and she wasn't ready to share the details. My mother told her she was always welcome whenever she wanted to talk.

One night, the ex-wife came over to discuss what had happened. It turned out her ex-husband had left her for another woman. Not so weird right? Happens all the time. As she continued her story, however, I couldn't believe what I heard. Turned out the ex-husband had been living a double life. He had another family! They didn't have children, but he had had another woman for the past fourteen years! Not just for some extra erotic activities. No, no! They actually had a life together, too. They traveled, went away on weekends, had Christmas parties with the family of the other woman, and so on. Nobody ever had had a clue! Nobody.

He kept it a secret all those years until he finally asked for a divorce because the kids were old enough, and he wanted to continue his life with the other woman.

Men can lie and play games, and some men are pretty good at it. My parent's friend was heartbroken by this deceit; her entire love life had been a lie. Even now, fourteen years or so later, she's still not over this.

That's one of the reasons I wrote this book. I want to give you an inside look into the mind of game-playing men, so you can try and recognize them and then decide whether to run away or try to make it work (although this is not advised).

There are many kinds of game players, but there's one recurring characteristic they all have. They'll be different than most other men you've met. They'll make you feel special, but more importantly, they will use certain strategies to make you believe *they* are special.

They will bring their A-game, deliberately show their alpha-male status, and other personality traits that women in general respond well to. You won't be the first woman they've practiced upon. Most game players have an actual playbook.

Game players love to be a challenge, to keep you guessing. They will add a great layer of mystery. When you ask him personal questions, in most cases, he will simply deflect those with humor. A game player will keep you on your toes and will keep the relationship exciting at all times. In some relationships, he'll be all you can think about.

Players are Great Marketers

Game players are great marketers. They know how to research, find out what you want, and then give it to you. However, they will spoon-feed it to you, so you keep coming back for more.

This marketer will also use influential techniques like social proof, scarcity, liking, similarity, and so on. More importantly, he's going to find out your love scars—how other men have hurt you or disrespected you in the past—and he'll present himself as the opposite of those bad men. He'll be the Doctor McDreamy who heals your love wounds.

It might sound theoretical and silly, but real game players will follow the handbook of a great marketer. They'll research you, question you (the target audience), discover your needs and wants, and then sell you on the idea they can fill those needs and wants. True game players will, of course, do this in a magical under-the-radar way; they will sell themselves to you without you ever knowing what's going on.

I'm not proud of it, but I've used these powers on two women. As a dating coach, I coach men as well, so I know a strategy or two. In these two separate occasions, I met women who found out what I do for a living and their first challenge for me was "So you think you can make any woman fall for you?" to which my response was: "Definitely not. I just know how to avoid messing it up with women who are at least slightly interested in me. I know how to raise their interest level." Both women, on separate occasions, challenged me, "Sure, but prove to me that you can seduce me. Say something that will seduce me." I explained that isn't how it works; "only famous men can make most women fall for them in an instant. I work under the radar. If I really want a woman, she might simply wake up one day and realize she has developed feelings for me. She won't see it coming."

Then we talked about other mundane things and had a great night. What both women didn't know, however, was that the game had already started for me. Every question I asked, everything I said, and the way I said it was a strategic choice with one goal in mind: make them fall for me. I don't feel too guilty since they both dared me. And I didn't apply any of these techniques on my long-term girlfriend whom I love very much.

It took me three weeks with the first woman and one single evening with the second woman. After our first kiss, I was able to say, "See? I told you so." They too had fallen for me, even though they should have known I was coming.

How did I do it? First of all, I noticed that I had passed the so-called physical attraction test. They thought I was cute; I could see it in their eyes and feel it in their body language. This is a crucial first step for every game player. Once they heard what I did for a living they had huge, defensive walls up to make sure I couldn't get to them. Those walls were easy to take down by using the standard game-player tricks. I showed them and told them exactly what they needed to hear to fall for me. And my game was different for each of those women, since their needs, wants, and flaws varied as well.

This is one of the many games men will try to play. In this book, I'll unveil how and why some men do this, so you can better protect your heart and your precious time.

Men who play games will in general seduce you by finding out what you need and want and then giving it to you. This includes making themselves seem more important or successful than they really are; they'll give you the feeling that you'll have a life filled with adventure, fun, and excitement with them (this can be true in some cases).

There's already one big clue, however, to be aware of. Game players will put in a lot of effort in the beginning of the relationship. They want to hook you on the line and get you on board. When you are on board, their efforts will greatly decrease.

When a man is playing games with you, you'll soon find out that you will be the one doing all the giving. The initiative will most often come from you, the effort will come from you, and he will do the absolute minimum to still get whatever he needs and wants from you. This might be sex, having a trophy woman, or even simply companionship.

Why Men Play Games With You

1. Because he can

I'm only thirty-four years old, but I'm old enough to have learned that most people will do what you let them get away with—especially men. Some men have childlike tendencies and need to be reminded of acceptable behavior. I'm not making excuses for men. There are bad types of men, who don't mean well. However, there are many guys who may simply not know any better.

If you only knew how many times my long-term girlfriend had to show me her boundaries, or explain why something I did wasn't acceptable in our relationship. Men need these discussions. We're not all psychics—we can't really read your mind. Therefore, it's highly encouraged to show someone else your owner's manual, so to speak. What hurts you, what do you find disrespectful or unacceptable behavior and so on. The goal however, is to always state this in an assertive manner, never by being mad.

If and when you don't stand up for yourself, men will start to walk over you simply because they can. If you have a female friend who is like this, I'm sure you'll see it's not just men who walk over her. Having a backbone is important in life, and you should never ever allow a man to play games with you.

I imagine you're thinking "Brian, *of course* I would never let him do this to me." And yet I've coached very intelligent women who were making this very mistake, because they were blinded by the love they felt for a certain man. What some women want is a man in their lives, someone who takes them out and makes them feel important. Game players know how to do this. It's part of their strategy.

Let's dig a little bit deeper into why you might be letting him to play games. I'm sure you're not like this, I don't want to insult your intelligence. That said, it always surprises me when I coach intelligent women who nevertheless make this mistake.

They let their man call all of the shots. They're available whenever he calls; they cancel other plans whenever he wants to go out. In general, they make *him* the top priority in their lives.

When a man feels this, this makes him think he's too good to fail. He'll think he can get away with anything, let alone with playing some games with you and not always being honest.

If a man knows a woman finds him the most important anything in his life, he just got the green light to invest a minimum of his time and efforts into the relationship, and still keep all of the positive rewards like sex, companionship when needed and so on.

2. Because he's unsure and waiting for someone better

This is a very common and hurtful reason why men might play games with you.

Here are some additional insights inside the mind of most men. Some men go out with women they find attractive and women they might love, even though they know she isn't the mother of his future children.
It's the best he could get at the time, but he's open and waiting for someone better. I know a lot of guys like these. They're in a relationship with a woman they love, but she has certain personality traits they know they can't stand for the long term. Or they think she's cute, just not cute enough for them. There might be a variety of reasons that make a man unsure.

A man who's unsure will give you hot and cold signals. When you distance yourself from him, he'll walk toward you. When you want to get closer, he will need some extra distance. This is one of the most obvious signs that he might be waiting for someone better.

Some men, however, are just unsure. They're not waiting for someone better; they're just not sure they want to be in a steady relationship. Some men who have a big fear of commitment might be playing games because of this. They want to keep you attached just enough so you won't break up with them. When they see signs you might run, they'll come closer and play games with you to keep you moving forward.

3. Because he's a nice guy

Contrary to what you may think, this type of man is the most dangerous one out there. Real nice guys are good at putting up a charade. You'll never know their true motives if you let yourself be hypnotized by their kindness.

A true nice guy is someone who tries to buy your love and your body with kindness. Those men often didn't receive enough attention or love from their own mothers while growing up. As a result, they've learned how to get at least some attention from their emotionally unavailable mother. The problem is they never unlearned it and keep doing it as adults. They try to get attention and love from everyone by being kind, nice, and good.

This might be a counter-intuitive topic for you. You may say, "Well, of course, I want a nice guy! Who on earth would want a bad boy?"

The problem is nice guys are not nice at all. They *pretend* to be nice to get something from you. This is/was the definition of a "game" as we've used throughout this book.

Here is an example:

When you're in a relationship with a normal man and he wants to have sex, he'll start to court you, touch you, kiss you, flirt with you, etc. When you're in a relationship with a Nice Guy and he wants to have sex, he'll do something nice for you. He will, for instance, buy you flowers or clean the kitchen in hopes that you will give him sex as a reward. He tries to buy your attention, your love, and your body by being good.

That's the game, the strategy, that Nice Guys follow. They'll be nice or try to make you feel good, but they always want your attention, your love, or your body in return.

Just to be clear, it's not because a guy is nice to you that he falls into this nice-guy camp. You'll recognize a Nice Guy when your gut starts to tell you he's playing games and he wants something from you in return for what he just did. It will feel as if everything has a hidden agenda. After a while, you'll grow tired of his predictability and childlike, attention-seeking behavior.

4. Because he doesn't respect himself or women

Men who don't respect themselves don't know what they want. They change their identity and/or their opinion faster than a chameleon can change colors. Men who don't respect themselves don't respect anyone else either. They don't care that the games they play might hurt you. To them, it's a kind of addiction. They want to dominate other people, hustle, and play games. This is what makes them feel powerful.

Bullies use the same strategy, by the way. They try to enhance their self-confidence and self-respect by picking on others. This is a ridiculously childish strategy.

5. Because he's a wimp

Some men are real cowards; they try to play it safe at all times. He never wants to rock the boat, take any risks, or do anything that would be outside of his comfort zone.

This might put them in the same category as the unsure men I previously discussed. They know they want someone else or better, but they're too wimpy to go after her, so they settle for what they think is less.

6. Because he's married

Surprisingly, I've coached a lot of women who fell for a committed man. There was something about him that made him attractive. I only have one piece of advice for these women: get out of there as fast as you can. **Treat him like you would any other vampire, because that's what he is. He will feed on you and dry you out emotionally before you know it.**

These men often play games, willingly or not, and will tell you things like:

- "The marriage is ending. I don't love her anymore, and I'll soon be ready to tell her I want a divorce." (In most cases, he won't do this. Sure, he's looking for some extramarital activities, but he won't leave her in most cases. Most often, he'll choose the security and the stability of his own marriage.)

- "I love you. I want to be with you, and I'll leave my wife soon." (You know, this does happen, but it doesn't make it any better. Would it be a good idea to be in a relationship with a guy who thought it was OK to cheat on his previous wife? Probably not.)

Married men who are open for a relationship or a fling cannot be trusted in any way. They are master players. They "game" their wives, and they will game you.

Don't be that woman. Don't wait for him. Don't listen to what he says, especially when he explains how bad his marriage is and his desire to leave her. He might not do it, and you don't want to be the other woman. This would put you in the weak position from the get go, where you constantly have to wait for him. That relationship will most probably fail anyway. You deserve so much better.

Types of Men Who Plays Games

1. The Player

The player plays because he wants to, because he can, and because some women let him. He is the least dangerous type of game-playing man. The reason is simple: you can see him coming from a mile away. He doesn't need to lie or play a lot of games (or any at all) to get women.

He might even communicate that he's a player and won't try to hide it. You'll see him flirt with other women and simply do whatever he wants. He might talk about the other women he's dating. He won't try to hide it. You'll see women waiting in line for his attention, his smile, a quick touch, a flirtatious gesture, or a conversation. Players have lots of options; they get lots of incoming date requests from other women (even intelligent ones who should know better).

If it's so easy to spot a player, why do so many women fall into his trap? This always intrigued me, and I've studied players and the women who fall for them in my early days as a relationship coach. I remember a beautiful and intelligent woman I was interviewing when I created one of my previous books. She told me she fell for players because it made her feel good. Players can pick from many women, and when he picked her that made her better than those other women (at least in her own mind).

There is some truth behind that. Some women see it as a nice compliment, an ego booster, when a player picks them over all the other women in his playbook. The big problem is that it's super easy to fall in love with a player.

The player himself is a man who knows his way around women. He knows how to charm them, how to be charismatic, emit positive energy, smile, dance, and seduce them with his positive energy. He loves it; he lives for it. Players attract women because they give them an ecstatic adventure—full of fun and positive energy. At least, that's what they want you to believe.

I have many player friends who have one mission in life: sleep with as many women as possible. When I studied players, I noticed their own behavior comes from some kind of insecurity. They need constant validation that they are good enough, and they need many women for this very reason. Women are like a drug to them. They just need a fix. They need variety, and eventually they want more and more.

Let me prove this further. You'll see that many successful men had a difficult childhood. They think they have something to prove, because their mom or dad never appreciated them enough. They were never good enough. As a result, they try to become wildly successful in business just to prove them wrong.

Well players have that mindset as well. The only difference is players use women as the prize; they measure their success by the amount of women they have "gotten." It makes them feel valuable.

This has some serious consequences if you ever want to have a relationship with a player. You cannot win. His hunger is insatiable. I'll never forget when one of my good-looking player friends in his early thirties had finally found the woman he was going to stay with forever. She was an intelligent lawyer, had a great supportive upper-class family, long legs, blond hair, a beautiful face, and killer body. When she looked at you, you couldn't help but feel warm and tingly inside. That relationship lasted about four months before my friend broke up with her.

His reason? "She was holding me back. I couldn't combine this relationship with going out, meeting other people, and having all of the female friends I have."

With the risk of sounding like a broken record: don't date a player. Don't try to change him, and don't wait for him to change. He won't.

You might be able to pin him down for a while if you're really good, but his hunger will soon kick in and turn your relationship into a heavy, daily struggle. "Use" a player for fun, if you need some. But don't fall for him. Since this is so hard, I suggest you keep players at bay at all times.

These are dangerous types of players for some women. I've had a lot of clients who thought they could eventually change him and make him see that they are wife-material. This type of player is mostly honest and upfront, especially about not being ready for a relationship. They clearly warn all the women they date that they won't want a relationship.... and yet, most of these women keep hanging on, hoping that he'll change his mind someday.

Don't try to pin down a player. It's OK to date a player, but please don't expect a future together. Don't wait for it, and don't try to change him. Take it as it is. If that's not enough for you, please move on and to avoid a lot of heartache.

2. The "I'm Not Sure What I Want" Guy

This is a very interesting fellow. This guy is not a player, since players DO know what they want: lots of women. This type of guy, Mr. Doubter as I'll call him, doesn't know what he wants. He's paralyzed and procrastinates about everything, especially about who to be in a relationship with.

Mr. Doubter loves the benefits of being single and the freedom that comes with it. And when I talk about men and freedom, please don't mistakenly think this is about "meeting other women." No, this freedom is about watching what he wants on TV, going to bed when he wants, waking up when he wants, and having the freedom to be wherever he wants whenever he wants with whoever he wants (think of his male friends, not just women).

Being in a relationship obviously limits that freedom a lot.

That said, Mr. Doubter loves to be in a relationship as well. He loves to have fun with a woman, having someone to talk to, travel with and enjoy all of the benefits of a relationship.

He simply doesn't know what to choose. He wants to have the best of both worlds. When you're in a relationship with this kind of guy, you'll be in trouble. He'll be hot and cold. One day he'll love to be with you, the next day you'll feel as if you're not wanted there. You're not wrong; this is how he actually feels, although he's probably not going to share this information with you and play games to hide it. That's exactly why your gut will still tell you something's wrong.

This guy will be the guy you'll want to ask, "Where is this going?" He won't know, and his evasive answers will probably drive you crazy. Truth is, he really doesn't know.

Some of the techniques I'll explain later on in this book will work very well on this kind of doubter. You'll need to lead him in such a way so that he still believes it was his own decision (that's the trick with most men, not just the game players). More on that later.

3. The Sexually Confused Guy (Gay or Straight?)

Ouch. Needless to say this is a dangerous type of man. In case I've just lost you here, trust me, these men do exist. I have met many of these men and even suspect one of my good friends to belong in this category.

I'll explain. One of my friends is really good with women and he always has been from the moment I met him. More than a decade later, we're both in our mid-thirties. He has a new girlfriend every month and attracts women like moths to a flame.

Women are his primary motivator. He's infatuated with them. With everything he does, he has one goal: to get more women. Even social media is a marketing outlet for him, where he carefully choses what he says and shows to reach his goal of getting more women.

Last year I was at a BBQ at his gorgeous and well-decorated house. While we we're all standing on the beautiful terrace looking at the sunset, I noticed something special. There were plenty of gorgeous women there. It was as if I was walking around on the set of a music video; beautiful women were everywhere.

Then I noticed something else. Out of every ten women, my friend had already had sex with at least six of them. The four others were there to get into his pants...eventually. I always wondered whether or not they knew they had all shared the bed with the same guy. I bet they did. He had all these women together to showcase how successful he was with the female gender. He adored them, and they adored him.

Then we started to work out together, him and me. We would work out and then end up talking about life, our jobs, cars, and women in the hot sauna that came with the fitness subscription. After a couple of times in the steam room, I noticed he always sat just a little too close to me. We were both naked, wearing only a towel around our midsection. Nothing ever happened, but I had a strange feeling that I never shook off. I'm sure you might know what I talk about, when a guy stands or sits just a little too close to you...

I started to wonder: "What if he's gay or fighting to not be gay? What if he's using all those women to avoid becoming gay? Like exposure therapy of some kind."

Since relationships and attraction are part of my job, I started to research this further and found out it isn't uncommon at all for gay men, who don't want to be gay, to try and get as many women as possible. Can you imagine a man, who would love to be straight, waking up in a gay body? Must be a tough situation.

There are different subtypes of these gay game players. Some will not be interested in sex with you; they will seem to be the perfect gentlemen! Giving you all of the benefits of a great relationship without the coming on too strong too soon part. They'll listen to you; they'll be really interested in what you have to say, in gossip, in fashion, etc..

At the other end of the spectrum, we find the sex addict who cannot get enough sex with as many women as he can simply to take his mind of the fact that he's more attracted to men. This guy simply wants to change his sexual preference that way.

I'm sure you've heard stories of married men who all of a sudden come out of the closet when nobody ever suspected it. It happens. And the games these men play are of the sneakiest kind.

How can you eventually spot this type of guy when you're in an actual relationship with him?

There are two major signs:

1. He'll start to cheat on you or flirt with other women, because he can't stop his "I need more women" drive.
2. He will be less and less interested in having sex with you. While your looks haven't changed and you're still taking care of your body, he doesn't seem to notice it; it doesn't arouse him anymore.

Other simple signs are his behavior. Does he spend more time in the bathroom than you? Is he more interested in shoes or fashion than you or women in general? And so on. When he's showing some "ideal girlfriend" behavior on top of the two major signs, then you'll know.

I realize I'm using stereotypes here, that's because we don't have a lot to go on. Like I said, this type of "gay player" is very good at playing games, his entire life is a lie, a charade.

4. The "I've Been Hurt Before" Guy

This guy, Mr. Hurt as I'll call him, has been hurt before and has been conditioned to fear women. Most men and women have been wounded before, but it left deep emotional scars for Mr. Hurt. Every new woman he meets automatically reminds him of all the painful moments he has experienced.

Here are some of examples of Mr. Hurt:

- The man who went through a divorce in the last five years
- The man who has been cheated on
- The man who never had a meaningful relationship because women keep rejecting him
- The man who has a serious fear of commitment because he's only dated clingy and needy women
- The man who had an experience with a woman that was so bad that he can't shut up about it, even to you, his new love interest

This is a difficult man to be in a relationship with, because he simply won't trust you. He won't give his everything. He'll be afraid to uncover something about you that will hurt him, or he'll be terrified that you'll notice something about him when he gets too close that will make you run away. This guy will play games as well for the simple reason that everything he does will be tentative. He won't give his all.

You'll recognize this type of guy when he says things like, "Let's take it slow. I love you, but I need us to go slow." or "I've had bad relationships in the past and need time to adjust."

The behavior of Mr. Hurt will be pretty clear. He'll simply be very tentative. You'll feel that he's holding back for some reason.

So what can you do about this? Try to be supportive, and do not pressure him. Time needs to heal his wounds. If you don't have time to wait, move on. He won't change any day soon, and his fear to commit will remain high for a long time.

5. The "I Don't Trust Women" Guy

This guy is comparable to Mr. Hurt. The big difference is he just doesn't trust women because, in his opinion, they are not honest toward him. They play games and have ulterior motives, according to him. This makes him a challenge to most women and thus, fairly attractive.

Examples of Mr. Notrust are:

- The man who has a lot of money and mostly meets gold-diggers
- The man who has been cheated on
- The man who has been lied to
- The man who had an emotionally unavailable mom

Mr. Notrust will play games with you because he won't give his all, and he will not value or respect you. This is dangerous, since this is exactly what might attract you on a subconscious level. Some women fall for men that represent this type of challenge. They want to change him and show him they are, in fact, good and trustworthy.

It's harder to spot Mr. Notrust. The best way is to verify whether he respects you. If he doesn't, even though you are the catch that I'm sure you are, it's possible that he doesn't value you, because he doesn't trust you. He will be in a continuous internal fight between giving himself to you and wanting to be single again, where everything is safe and where he cannot be hurt.

6. The "I'm Waiting for Someone Better" Guy

When you're in a relationship with a guy who makes you insecure about the future of the relationship, chances are it's this type of guy. This is a very dangerous type of man because he will play his game perfectly if he's any good at it.

Here are some signs that you're dealing with a guy who's waiting for someone better:

- He doesn't introduce you to people who are important to him like his friends, family, or colleagues. He finds excuses not to invite or include you: "Oh honey, you wouldn't like it there anyway."
- He doesn't want to talk about "where this is going." He deflects this question.
- One day he's hot for you, the next day he's cold.
- He's often very busy and not only puts his professional life above you, but

> other activities and hobbies are more important than you too (most of the time).
> - You have a gut feeling that something's wrong, especially since his actions are not compatible with the words he's using.

This last item is an important sign. I've always said you should never listen to a man's words—only look at his actions. This is one of the ways this type of man will unveil his true identity. He might say he loves you or sees a future with you, but his actions might prove the opposite when he's not ready to take the relationship to the next level or when he's simply not including you in his life.

Words are easy. It takes no effort at all to say anything. Actions are harder, much harder, and should be more important when you're trying to figure out what your man is all about.

7. The "My Daddy Never Loved Me" Guy

This guy comes in many forms and flavors and will be dangerous for your emotional well-being. This guy can be a player or anyone of the other categories, but he has one common denominator: he has something to prove! He wasn't valued by his father (or parents) while growing up and is still dragging that self-esteem complex with him. It will never go away.

This is the guy who

- Saw his daddy leave while he was growing up
- Had a dad who neglected him
- Had a dad who was not emotionally available
- Had divorced parents where most time was spent with the mother
- Had brothers or sisters who got all of the parental attention while growing up (and later on)
- Didn't have a real father figure for any other reason

Mr. Nodaddy has some serious emotional issues. Since nobody showed him, he doesn't know how to be a man, what it means to be a man, or how to behave like a man. This gives him some identity issues. The only way he knows how to be a man is to be as wildly successful as possible and to have as many women as humanly possible, on top of a successful career.

This man has the type-A personality and wants be the best. He will take you on a nice rollercoaster ride with highs and lows, and you'll never know where you stand. It's as if you're competing with many invisible enemies—other women, his job, and so on. He has so much going on in his life that it's truly hard to keep up.

The strange thing is that this guy can give you a romantic, movie-like relationship. But one thing is for sure, there won't be a happy ending. When you're happy with this guy, it simply means the story isn't finished yet.

That's the downside. He can change in the blink of an eye. One day you can be on a romantic getaway with him, only to hear that he wants to move on the next day.

So how can you recognize this guy? He's too much of everything. He'll be very successful or try to be, he'll be super romantic and do things you could only dream of. That's when your alarm bells should go off. If it's too good to be true...it is.

One of the women I recently coached met a Mr. Nodaddy recently. He was the prince charming she had been waiting for all her life. She was forty; he was fifty-one. He was a very successful and still good-looking man, Clooney type. He showered her with gifts, took her on a trip with a private plane, and then came the cherry on the pie when he proposed.

She was ecstatic! Finally! After all of the hard moments in her life, the good times would begin. She, however, failed to realize it was all going too fast and too well. They had only known each other for four months!

You guessed it. About a month later, Mr. Nodaddy changed his mind, cancelled the wedding, broke up with her, and became even more successful (in his own mind at least) by replacing my client with a younger version. True story.

Should you avoid this guy? Well, only if you're looking for something serious. If you want to have fun and have a great short-term experience, by all means, go for it! Great vacations end at some point, and if you can live with that, go ahead and enjoy them. Simply don't fall in love with him, and don't believe a word he says about the future. Enjoy the moment, because there probably won't be a future. He'll nevertheless treat you like a queen as long as it lasts.

8. The Child

Most men act like children every now and then. I do, and I know it. Some men, however, get stuck in their teens and never grow up. The last time they evolved was when they were 16 or so; they still have the exact same type of personality.

The child is the type of man who wants to have fun all the time, who's afraid of responsibilities, who loves adventure, who doesn't have a plan, who is often not successful and earns just enough to have fun in life. If he is successful and found a way to have fun and earn a lot, he won't have any savings since every week is lived like there won't be a next. His life revolves around three things: his friends, his hobbies, and sports. It won't be about you.

This is a dangerous type of game player because he can be very attractive. Wasn't it Cindy Lauper who sang, "Girls just want to have fun?" He's full of fun, positive energy, and he won't be stiff and serious like most other men. He's the life of the party, and people love to be around him. Being with him raises your dopamine levels and makes you feel like you're a kid as well. When is the last time you had fun like a kid? It sure feels good every now and then.

This guy is an adventurer. He'll take you on that adventure; he'll have fun with you until he embarks on the next adventure with another woman. Yes, he does like variety, of course; all children do.

Watch out for this guy. Most of my clients who've dated one of these types of men think it wasn't worth it, looking back at it afterward.

9. The Pickup Artist

This is a special breed of men. You'll mostly find them below thirty-five years of age. Pickup artists are often nerds and/or losers who got fed up with not being able to attract women at all. They have no social skills, don't know how to talk to women, let alone attract one. They always end up as the best friend, at best. In most cases, they were socially awkward in their teens and twenties.

Until the late '90s, these men were doomed to live lonely lives, or find a woman who couldn't find anyone better. In the early 2000s, when the Internet started to flourish, everything changed. All of a sudden, websites became available where you could buy a membership and learn how to seduce women. These men weren't taught to use the good old tricks men have had for ages. No, these pickup artists were taught terms like peacocking (showing off in very influential ways) or a tactic of giving you a compliment first only to add something negative afterward (e.g., Wow! You look nice in that dress. Too bad your purse doesn't seem to match it.). They employ a whole range of psychological strategies and tactics to attract women. They manipulate women.

And you know what? It worked. Not all the time, of course, and not on every woman, but these pickup artists turned attraction into a science, and in their true nerd style, they became masters at it.

Should you worry about a pickup artist? Probably not, unless you're the type of woman who sleeps with a guy after the first date. Their magic might still be working then, but when you do step into a relationship with any of these self-proclaimed artists, their masks will quickly drop and their true lack of self-confidence will be revealed. They are very good in the early stages of a relationship, introducing themselves to you, flirting, and getting your phone number. Once you're out on a date with them, the magic should soon start to fade away.

Two Reasons Why Men Won't Commit

Hollywood has long wanted us to believe that fairytales and happy endings are real. Unfortunately, they aren't always. There is a quote from the movie *Mr. and Mrs. Smith*, "HAPPY ENDINGS are just STORIES THAT haven't FINISHED YET."

In general, most women and men are looking for that perfect relationship, for "the one." Most women are looking for their Prince Charming—someone who will sweep them off their feet and make them feel secure, safe, and loved for the rest of their lives.

Is it possible that's what you're looking for as well? That security and unconditional love Prince Charming could, should, and would provide?

I don't believe in fairy tales and the picture Hollywood tries to portray to us. I'm sorry if what I am about to say will make you angry or upset, but I don't want to hold back. I believe you'll have a better love life when you truly understand reality, instead of the fairy tales we're projected by Hollywood.

Dr. Helen Fisher, famous for her research and TED talk about relationships, is one of many scientists who keep proving and confirming that we're just animals, even in love. We're simply reacting to chemicals and hormones in our bodies. Geoffrey Miller, another researcher in this field and author of *The Mating Mind*, taught me that most of what we do has one goal: procreate, spread our genes, and create off spring.

This system works differently for men than it does for women. Men have it easy. To spread their genes, they need to make as many babies as humanly possible, that's what their body wants. And since their sperm factory keeps running well over their fifties, they could indeed make a lot of babies if contraception didn't exist (and if their dating and seduction skills were perfect). They not only could make a lot of babies, they actually would. Every time a man would have sex with a fertile woman, a baby might have been conceived since, in nature's eyes, condoms and the pill don't exist. Men don't need to be really picky; they have an abundance mindset, an endless supply of little spermatozoids.

That's one of the reasons why men hate to commit too soon or cannot appreciate the reality that they will never be with another woman than the one they're currently with. It's against their nature, against their instincts.

Women, on the other hand, have a totally different natural mindset. Your supply IS limited. You only have a certain amount of fertile years, a limited amount of eggs. That's OK. That's the way nature intended it. When you are pregnant, you will not be able to make any new babies for almost a year. And when that cute baby is born, you'll get other hormones that bond you to that baby and make him/her the most important thing in your life, often more important than yourself. Since we are humans, you'll also need to care for your child for at least 12-16 years before your kid would at all be able to make it on his/her own in this world.

That's quite the investment, of course—an investment men don't need to make. They don't have that mother-baby bond you would have.

I exclude the fact that most men have more than just their natural instincts and will, of course, rationally love you and the baby. They should want to stay with you for a couple of years, but nature will only make them stay for about three years. That's when their own hormones will change again, when the hormonal bond to you and the child will be broken and when they'll start looking for something new. The reason is that nature thinks the child will be OK with his mother after three years, and it's thus OK to find a new woman to make babies with.

Let me emphasize that this is what nature wants. Most men DO stay longer than three years, because they decide to and because they decide to fight their instincts to find someone new. It's not a coincidence by the way that most little brothers and sisters are made a few years after the first child. This is a strategy some couples use to renew the natural bond for a couple of years.

Again, if this is upsetting you, then I'm sorry. But it's important to understand this reality. Women who believe in the fairytale of endless, unconditional love are the ones who have the most hurtful and troublesome love lives. Reality keeps proving them wrong.

So you can see that for a woman, it's crucial to find the right man. A woman can only make a limited amount of babies, so nature wants her to make them with the right man—one with good genes and one who will stay as long as possible to help raise the children.

So romance, love, and attraction are nature's way of playing with our hormones with only one goal in mind: procreation. This is one of the crucial reasons to not have sex too soon with a man. Another hormone, oxytocin, is at fault here. The second you let him arouse you and intimately touch you, your body will release oxytocin and other hormones that will make you bond with him.

Your body doesn't know there's such a thing as contraception. When you have sex with a man, nature thinks that you might become pregnant so it's crucial, for the sake of your offspring, that you fall for this guy and try to keep him around until the child has become self-sufficient. Our society has evolved, but our body is still stuck in the Paleo area. Our bodies are not up to speed with contraception and all of the changes we've seen the last 100 years. Don't let oxytocin fool you. It can make you bond with a guy who's not good for you, just because you had sex with him.

These hormones are also the reason why most women love to cuddle and talk after sex; they want to stay together and be intimate. The male thinks, "OK, good job. Now onto the next priority of the day" as he's ready to get up and continue with his day. All men have this, not just the game players. Men like myself get up and get some work done, or fall asleep. Game players, on the other hand, have other ideas and plans, often involving the next woman.

We're not just animals; the difference between animals and humans is that we don't blindly follow our emotions and instincts. When you make a bear mad, he will attack. You can't reason him out of it; you can't discuss this with him, even if you would talk bear-lingo. Animals simply follow their instincts. We humans do not. We can rationalize anything. Nevertheless, most people are still greatly influenced by their emotions.

So why am I explaining all of this? Because I want you to understand there's no such thing as your soul mate, your prince charming. In fact, multiple men can fall into that category. You can be with a guy who is the one for you, your soul mate, only to love another man even more, ten years down the road. And that's the good and important news.

This is crucial information since some women treat their love interest as if he's the ONLY one. They try to move heaven and earth to get him, keep him, change him, and so on because they share one belief: I'm never going to find anyone better than him.

That's simply not true, and this makes them waste precious time if they're with the wrong type of man. This female behavior can even push the right type of man away. Most men get scared when they feel they're the most important anything in your life.

So why is that? Well, in short, it's because this makes men realize three things:

- They have you. Fully. There's no challenge left. (Men love a challenge; they need it.)
- If it was this easy to get a great woman like yourself, could he upgrade and even get a better one? Men often want more and more.

-   They start to realize this is it for them.
    Since the challenge is gone they'll need
    to settle down with you. But what about
    all of the other women and
    opportunities out there?

As long as you'll stay at least a bit of a challenge,
you'll keep his attention focused on not losing
YOU. Men can only think about one thing at a time,
seriously. As a result, he won't be thinking about
other women, about the walls moving in on him, or
his fear of commitment. I apologize if all of this
seems quite harsh, but this again is simply the
reality.

On top of that, some women have certain
behaviors that keep a man reluctant. These
behaviors make him unsure about her and the
relationship and could force him to endure her,
while he's waiting for someone better.

Here are some of these avoidable reasons:

a. Neediness
The biggest reason he won't commit has
everything to do with neediness. The more you
NEED him, the less he'll want to commit. No
matter what a great catch you are.

It's OK to want a man. It's not OK to need a man. Men can smell this desperation a mile away, and they're honestly scared of needy women. You'd be too. Just imagine being with a guy who really needs you, who's scared you might leave him someday, and who keeps trying not to lose you. I'm sure you've met men like this and you had an icky reaction to them.

Women who need a man are often women who can't stand to be alone. They don't think they are enough, and they continuously need a man in their lives. The phrase "You complete me" comes to mind. Without their man, they don't feel whole. Once these women finally get a great guy, all they can think about is "I hope I won't wake up and realize this is a dream. I need to do ANYTHING I can to prevent losing this guy."

Men are afraid to commit to a woman who shows signs of needing him. It freaks them out and gives them a lot of fear. Men, on the other hand, are super attracted to women who don't need them.

Did you ever notice that in most cases, you don't want the men who want you? You want the men who seem less interested? If you could only switch it around... If you could only make the man you wanted as crazy in love with you as the men you're not interested in at all. That's not a coincidence. When you're not interested in a guy, you'll try to be nice, but you'll keep your distance. If you don't turn him down hard, he'll see you as a challenge. He might fall harder and harder for you because he still thinks he has a shot and you're simply playing hard to get.

Now that's exactly the type of behavior you should show the guys you DO want. Just pretend they're the nice guy you're totally *not* interested in. Show them the exact same behavior you would give these nice guys who you try to let down easily and see what that gives. You'll be very surprised.

Men always want what they cannot fully get.

b. Emotional Stability

Men fear emotionally unstable women. As a guy, we've all had a relationship with an ex who was emotionally unstable. She may be happy one minute and then boom, all of sudden, she gets mad while the man is wondering where the landmine is that he just stepped on.

I've been there, too. It's scary, and we, men, are super afraid to commit to living next to a minefield where we have to watch our steps with everything we do or say.

I realize it's often very hard to remain emotionally stable when you suspect your guy might be playing games with you. But this is all the more reason to be stable! Your emotional instability will only turn his lies and games further on, if only to avoid upsetting you or stepping on a landmine that would make you mad or yell at him.

Let me repeat this since it's so important. If a man is already playing games with you, he will play even more games and fake it even more if you nag or get jealous or upset at him.

Be stable, and use some of the other strategies you find in this book to make him show his real cards. Don't get mad at him. This will only make it worse, especially since even a good guy will not want to commit to a woman who takes him on an emotional rollercoaster.

Men simply cannot handle emotions as well as women can.

What Do Men want From You?

Before I dive into this chapter, let's talk about women first. Most women look for stability and some form of security in their man. They don't want to go at it alone and love to share their life, their stories, their problems, and so on with a great man, a life partner. They also look for security, be that financial security or emotional security. They would love to get unconditional love from a man and have everything under control, so everything stays the same forever. Happily ever after, forever and ever.

Men are, of course, different. I'll discuss many aspects that are important to them in what follows. How important one of these aspects is to a man will differ from one man to the next. Here are two elements that are important to every man:

1. For most men, at least for the first couple of years in the relationship, sexual attraction and actually getting sex is most important. Men love to look at their woman and think, "Wow, she's so hot. I can't believe I have her and can have sex with her whenever she doesn't have a headache" (I'm sorry, I couldn't leave that one on the table ;-)). This is what drives most men at first. It will remain an important driver throughout the entire relationship, regardless of your age.

2. This comes in a close second and becomes more and more important the longer the relationship lasts. It's one word: team. Every successful man needs and wants a strong woman by his side; he wants someone who makes him a better man and helps him achieve goals he couldn't have achieved without her. Men can be looking for emotional support, practical support, a talking board, and someone who stands by him no matter what.

I once had a neighbor who was in a very fulfilling relationship with his wife. They had been married for over twenty years, had two lovely daughters, and all was perfect. I know since I never heard a single fight, not even a raised voice, and I could see they were operating as a great team. My investigative nature made me question my neighbor about his perfect relationship and to illustrate what a great team they were, he gave me this weird but striking example:

"Well, Brian, if I would take a gun right now and shoot you in the face. You'd be dead. If my wife would walk in ten minutes later while your corpse is still on the floor, she wouldn't panic. She would say, 'George, I'm sure you had your reasons to kill Brian. What did he do and what should we do next to take care of this?'" In other words, she would stand by his side, no matter what.

A man who knows he has the support of his woman, her full support, can go out into the world and become all he can be. On a side note, most men are not sexists; he wants you to go out and be all you can be as well, and he will support you. This is not a "woman by the stove" and "is dinner ready yet?"" situation.

Game players find these two aspects very important as well. They, however, have a hidden agenda. They want a maximal ROI (return on investment). They'll try to invest as little time and effort in you as humanly possible, only to get the highest return possible.

For most types of game players, the ideal woman is a woman who:

- Looks super-hot and takes care of her body at all times. She's the most perfect version of herself at all times.
- She's ready to give him sex and other pleasures whenever he sees fit, whenever his batteries need to be recharged. She's there for him whenever he needs him and is OK with the fact that he often won't have time for her at all.
- She doesn't complain that he'll still want to go out there in the world and be wildly successful, or at least have as much fun as he can while not really paying her too much attention or giving her support (just the bare minimum to get the first two items of this list).

And so on. As you surely imagined, most game players have no respect for women at all.

After the physical aspect of attraction, emotional attraction is also important to game players and normal men. As you might have heard me explain before, physical or sexual attraction is all about your body and your looks. This is where he'll want to touch and kiss you. Emotional attraction, on the other hand, is where he'll want to be with you, talk to you, share his ideas and what happened during his day.

Long-term relationships are built on a mixture of emotional and physical attraction. Flings and extramarital relationships are often built on physical attraction alone.

Some form of game players can need this emotional attraction part a lot. Nice Guys, Mr. Nodaddy and Mr. Notrust types of men have an emotional barrel to fill. Problem is, there are leaks in the barrel, so regardless of how much time and effort you put into them, and it will never be enough. You can't win this game.

These men might for instance become jealous or mad whenever you don't act or behave the way they think you should have reacted. They constantly need your emotional support, since they didn't get it enough from mommy and/or daddy when they were growing up. They never learned to deal with it and move on.

Will a Game Player Never Want a Long-term Relationship?

Some game players will never want a long-term relationship, because they have psychological problems. They might want to give it a try, but the relationships will fail because their inner demons will always come to the surface. Mr. Nodaddy is one of those. He will always be fighting his inner demons for the rest of his life. As a result, he won't be able to spend enough time or attention on his partners.

In the early 2000s, there was a show on E! called Dr. 90210 where a certain Dr. Rey suffered from this problem. For as long as he participated in this reality show, you could see he was always trying to achieve super results as a surgeon, as a martial arts black belt, as a this and that. His wife, in the meantime, was at home complaining about the fact he never gave her enough attention. For as far as we could see as a viewer, she was right.

Some game players will try and fail. Others will never want to go for real long-term relationships in the first place. That might make you wonder: what type of woman do they want to commit to on the long term?

I see it happen sometimes, a player who went from one woman to the next only to all of a sudden find the woman of his dreams and settle down with her, have babies, a dog, and white-picket fences. Is that weird, or what?

Most game players have a large list of what they want in a woman. And they'll start to meet as many women as possible, go out with them, date them, and test them in order to find one who checks off all the boxes on the list.

Some women will be good enough for the sexual activities alone, other will be worth a shot, until she does something that's a big no no—something that scares him away.

I still have to suggest you stay away from game players for this reason alone. If you've read my book, *Are You Scaring Him Away*?, you know there are plenty of behaviors that can scare a man away. Those men are normal men, great catches. It's hard enough with normal men. Game players, however, are even more difficult to keep, with a much smaller return on your investment. You could try to be the perfect girlfriend or wife all you want, chances are it will never be enough for the game player.

Additional Signs that He's Playing Games With You

Although every man can wear a mask and not be totally honest with you, every now and then, game players share a set of signs or red flags that will reveal their true intentions.

Most of these signs will actually prove that he doesn't see a future with you and he's playing a game so he can keep using you for as long as he needs. Here are the most important signs and red flags:

> a. He's hiding you from other people like his friends or coworkers.

This is a major one. When a game player doesn't introduce you to his family, best friends, or coworkers, there's something wrong. He doesn't need to do this right away, of course, but when you're more than two months into the relationship, and he's never invited you to join him at gatherings where you'd normally be welcome, then treat this as a major red flag. He'll use excuses like "You wouldn't like it there, honey" and so on.

A big red flag is when there is a professional get-together where everyone can bring their partners and he doesn't invite you.

There are multiple reasons for him to hide his girlfriend. The most hurtful one is that he doesn't think she's pretty or interesting enough; he's afraid of the remarks and opinions from his friends, colleagues, or family. He's afraid to be seen with her.

When this man gets himself a Ferrari or a Porsche, he'd start to show off and invite all of his friends and colleagues to have a look or make sure they'd know he has this fine piece of machinery. He would take it to most parties and get-togethers and ask his friends if they want a ride.

Well, not to objectify women, but most men would do the exact same with their girlfriends; he would love to show her off to the world. When he doesn't do this, something's wrong. He's supposed to be proud of the fact that he got you to go out with him or be in a relationship with him.

Another reason why a game player might not invite his girl is the simple fact that he knows he won't stay with her for long. What's the point in introducing her to everyone, only to have to explain later on why he broke up with her? This is a major problem for some of my player friends I have. Every time they had a new girlfriend, his friends and I would get attached to her and become friends only to later hear he broke up with her and she wouldn't be joining us anymore. We would miss her too, of course, and ask about her. I remember one of my old friends having a relationship with a certain Jessica. During a group get-together a few months later, we were introduced to Sarah, his new girl for that weekend (while he was still together with Jessica as well). We didn't know what to say, felt pity for Sarah, and were afraid to run our mouths.

All of these examples motivated me to write this book for you, to unveil the truth about some men.

b. He's avoiding locations close to his home or work.

This is a major and not-so-obvious red flag. Most women don't notice this and don't see it on their radar.

So why would a man avoid locations close to his home or work? He's too afraid to be seen with his new woman by other women he's already dating, or by other people he knows who could run their mouth and give him away. Someone may say, "This must be Jessica!" Sarah, the woman he took out, probably wouldn't be too pleased to hear this.

Even worse, imagine how busted a game player would be if he takes woman B out to a great restaurant, only to bump into women A whom he took there a week before...

c. You're not that welcome at his place.

Some men are nesters. They can't wait to start a family, get kids, and create the nest where everybody will live and have fun together as a happy family. Game players, however, will not want to share their home base with just about anyone, especially not with a woman they see no future with.

There are a variety of reasons for this. One of them is the fear of a stalking woman. I've had my fair share of stalkers as well, and I'm not even a real game player. Women kept showing up uninvited just to say hi, when I had ended the relationship months earlier.

Other reasons might be that he's just not ready to share his intimate world with you; he's afraid you'll notice his wall of fame with pictures of all the women he has dated, or other telltale signs of his game playing.

If you've been with him for more than a month and you've never seen his place, add that as a major red flag.

> ### d. You're investing a lot more time and effort into the relationship than he is.

This is a clear red flag. It's totally normal that the investment is not always in a perfect equilibrium, but in general, who's investing the most of his/her time and efforts? Are you a nuisance to him? Is he keeping his investment to a strict minimum?

A clear and important sign of this is when you're dealing with a texter or an e-mailer. Is he taking the time to actually call you, talk to you, or does most of his communication come in the form of a quick text message, e-mail, or other form of textual communication? That's how game players can limit their time investment, while maintaining relationships with as many people (or women) as possible.

In the movie *Ghosts of Girlfriends Past*, Matthew McConaughey breaks up with multiple women at once over a multi-person Skype call. Efficiency is key for a player. That is not to say that every game player has relationships with multiple women at once, of course. It just explains how important he thinks his girl really is, compared to all of the other things in life (his work, friends, family, hobbies, football, etc.).

Also look at who's adapting and changing his/her schedule to meet up, to go out on a date, or do something fun together. A true game player won't change his schedule for a woman he's not really that interested in.

It again comes down to watching his actions, never his words. Words are easy. But is he putting in an effort when you look at his actions? Do his actions clearly show love and devotion? If they don't, please consider this to be a major red flag.

e. Lies and inconsistencies

A true game player has a lot to hide. This is difficult for him. He needs to remember what lies he told you. He'll, for instance, need to make sure you can't find or touch his phone (he won't even let it lay around, since you might notice another woman texted or tried to call him). True players, the first kind I discussed earlier in the book and the least bad kind because they are upfront about their personality, might not even put in the effort to hide this. The fact that many women are in contact with them is a plus for them; it raises their perceived importance and challenge.

The lies and inconsistencies flag can be added when your gut tells you that something is wrong on more than a couple of occasions. When you catch him telling a white lie more than twice, add this as a major red flag; he's probably a game player.

How to Force Him to Show His Cards

When you've had it with his games and you want to know what the future holds, you'll have a couple of strategies you can deploy. Let's start with what *not* to do.

Don't give him an ultimatum, don't nag, and don't be mad at him. This will only enhance his game-playing mode, and he will just keep his cards close to his chest. Look at his actions, and don't listen to his words. His words don't mean anything, especially when he's the type of man who plays games.

The strategy I'm about to explain is risky, because you might lose him. Please realize that this is OK. I'm sure you'll only use this test whenever you need to be really sure, so you can go on with your life—with or without him.

There's one thing that will make a game player run away fast and that's a committed future with the woman he's not being honest with. In my other books, I explain many strategies of what not to do to avoid giving a man the infamous fear of commitment. Well here, we'll actually try to give him this fear. If he's not playing games and does see a future with you, he won't budge and will stick around, even though he might feel some fear. He'll embrace that fear since he doesn't want to lose you. He'll see that fear as a temporary disadvantage, something that will soon go away.

If he does run or break up with you, then at least you'll know. He was playing a game and didn't want to put in any effort to make it work.

Here's the strategy: talk about the future, a future together. Don't ask him if there is a future with you. Never ask "Where is this going?" to any man, especially a game player, since this will only make him lie more. Simply state some facts about a future together like, "That is a nice house. I can see us living in a house like this in the future." His reaction doesn't matter yet. A player can still play games while thinking, "Let's keep her happy until I find someone else to live in *that* house with." The goal is for you to start making more and more statements like this. Simply say something about a future together.

This will raise the fear to commit in any man, but most quickly in men who are playing games with you and who do not see a future at all.

Keep this up for a couple of weeks, and a true game player will start to make mistakes. His behavior toward you will start to change. He'll become more distant. You might catch him on little white lies (or even big ones). He might start to use excuses and dismiss a future together, too.

Then, when you're sure his behavior has changed, ask him, "Honey, are you all right? You seem different the last couple of weeks?" His answer will tell you everything. Here are the possible outcomes:

1. It's possible you never had to ask him the question at all, because he does see a future with you and would love to be with you forever and ever.

2. Even non-game playing men will start to feel some fear of commitment because of your strategy. I know I would, especially if this is just a recent or fresh relationship. But a normal man will be upfront about this and will communicate with you. In this case, he'll honestly say that he's got some fear to commit and that you made him feel a little weird after making those remarks about a future together. This is a red

flag. It's possible this relationship is going nowhere, but at least he's honest and not playing games.

3. The true game player will behave differently. He'll try to convince you nothing is wrong! What a lie. Something obviously is because you deployed this strategy and actually saw his behavior change. He is feeling that something is wrong, but he doesn't want to talk about it or be open and honest toward you. In this case, chances are you're dealing with a man who falls into one or more of the game-playing categories.

   As I'm sure you know, open and honest communication is an important cornerstone in any healthy long-term relationship. This guy has just proven he's not honest, at least for now, and prefers to wear a mask.

4. It's also possible you never get to ask him the question because he already ran away. "Oh honey, wouldn't that be a great house to live in in the future? ...honey? ...honey, where are you?" Well, at least you'll know he wasn't in it for the long term.

Is He Willing to Go the Extra Mile?

Say you have your doubts, but you don't want to use the strategy from the previous chapter because it is indeed an all-or-nothing strategy. It's quite risky. Are there less powerful strategies that will still test him? Sure there are.

a. Take a step back and see how he responds.

An obvious, but very efficient and difficult strategy is to take a step back, at least mentally. Stop talking about a future together. Start treating the relationship as if it will end soon, and take a step back to give him more space. Then, see how he responds to it.

Do not communicate this strategy to him, and definitely do not explain why you're doing this. The goal is to see his natural reaction to your changes.

In general, when you take a step back, a man who loves you and wants to be with you will care and will pursue you more. He'll ask what's wrong and start to increase his chase and his efforts (even if you're already in an established relationship). A game player will simply not care. He will let it die off slowly and will not change his behavior at all. He might not even be aware that you took a step back.

To make sure he notices, take it one step further.

> b. Make other things more important than him and see how he responds.

For many women, their man or guy is the most important person in the world (until they have babies). This sounds great, but actually isn't. A man will get scared when you make him the center of your life—above and beyond everything and everyone.

Is that what you do? When you're really in love with a man, does he become your "everything"? If so, that's not your fault; it's your natural instinct. That said, it's better to take a step back. Although he can be really important to you, you should make sure that you have other very important aspects in your life. This will keep the challenge alive for him. He'll need to keep respecting you and keep putting in the effort to make sure he can keep you.

Since you want to check whether your man is playing games or not, you'll need to take it one step further. He needs to lose his top position in your world.

So many women are too available. They follow his schedule and are simply happy to be around him. These are the women who might be in a relationship with a game player, because they let him play those games, as discussed earlier in this book.

The strategy here is to find some activities that you'll start to find really important (he needs to perceive that you think they are really important to you, even if they're not and you'd rather be with him). We're going to play a game with the game player. Take look at this example:

"Hey babe, can I come over tomorrow? We can watch a movie or something?" he asks.

"Sure, great! Come over any time you want. Do you want me to cook you dinner first?" the old you says.

"Actually no, tomorrow is not a good day. I already made plans with friends. What about next week on Tuesday?" the new you says.

"Wow. Who's she meeting? Am I on the way out? Did I do something wrong? What on earth could be more important than me? The king of this universe?" he will think.

If he's a game player, that's exactly what he'll think. No woman has ever thought something or someone else was more important than him. That's great, because this will give him the feeling that you're slipping away. Even though you're not doing anything wrong here, let's be honest. It's totally OK to say no and have plans with other people.

You're simply decreasing his value. He becomes less important. As a result, if he has feelings for you, YOUR value will rise. You'll create a challenge, and he'll start to work harder for you.

This is honestly a good strategy in every type of relationship you could possibly be in, with any type of man. Make sure you have plenty of things he needs to compete with. Don't center your entire life and happiness around him. I realize you might not be making this mistake, but you'd be surprised of how many great and intelligent women I've coached who did exactly this, blindsided by the love they felt for a man.

Men don't like this. They need a challenge. They only value things, jobs, money, and relationships they had to work for. Men want to earn what they get.

Strategies to Get Him

Whenever you've determined you're with a man who's playing games with you, you should run and never look back.

I know love can make us blind; I've been there, too. You might have thoughts like "Yeah, Brian, but he's really the man of my dreams. I've met so many men...but none like him. I want him and no one else." We'll deal with that kind of thinking later in this book. I'll first help you to still try to get him, if that's important to you, even though I don't advise it.

Make him see you as his girl.

It's crucial he sees you as "his girl." This is the girl he wants to protect at all costs. Real men want to protect their woman. This is a natural instinct. He'll want to care for you and provide for you if you treat him with respect. A king always wants to take care of his queen.

"His girl" is the girl he wouldn't ever want to replace. When I see pictures of my long-term girlfriend and other women, regardless of how beautiful those other women are, I'd always want to go home with her, my girl. I don't have a doubt in my mind about this. For me, she's always the most attractive one.

"His girl" is the girl he respects very much. This means he would never think of lying to her. If you're dealing with a game player, this one will be difficult. He's a natural liar and often doesn't know any better.

You can make him see you as his girl by being feminine, while never being needy or clingy. Most men want a strong, feminine woman. Emotional stability is key here. Women who constantly go from high to low and lash out and get jealous over nothing will never be "his girl."

Strong, feminine women are different. They have great hobbies, great friends, and thus don't center their lives around their man. This, by definition, will never make them needy or clingy since their happiness doesn't come from one person.

Men are very visual. When your guy first walked up to you, it wasn't because you had such a great personality. It's because you were visually appealing to him. He only found out about your personality later on; he honestly didn't care about it at first. We can use this visual approach to make him see you as his girl.

This is again where your other activities come into play. You'll need hobbies and activities that do not involve him. When he then later sees pictures of you having fun, his mind will visually start to define you as his girl. That's what men do. He will be looking into your world and define you as his girl, especially when he sees you having fun, unrelated to him. The simple fact of him seeing a Facebook picture of you and other people having fun without him might trigger this system.

There's another strategy that I don't endorse that will help him see you as his girl as well. And that's when you'd make him jealous. When he sees you talk to other men, he'll have the "hey, that's MY girl" reaction. This is OK if you didn't do it deliberately to make him jealous. It's, however never a good idea to use this as a conscious strategy, since that would be playing games with him, of course. A good relationship of any kind can never be built on games, period.

Make him feel that you're ready to walk away when not respected.

Men are like kids. When they can get away with something, they'll do it. As I mentioned earlier in the book, he'll go as far as you let him. It's crucial that you show him the line in the sand he should never cross.

One of those obvious lines is respect. He should always, always treat you with respect. Never ever accept anything less. You'd be surprised how many intelligent catches I've coached who settled for less and hoped he would change; they thought he was just having a rough period in his life that would eventually pass. It won't.

He can't respect you if you don't respect yourself enough to DEMAND to be respected. Demand might not be the right word here, since you're, of course, never going to actually ask for respect. The strategy is much simpler. Whenever he does something that's not really respectful, withdraw and make him less important. Be less available, put more time and effort in activities that do not involve him, steer your life away from him.

Never ever punish a man by being mad at him. This will always backfire. Remember, men are like kids and the best way to punish a kid is to ignore him until he turns around. Getting mad only delivers short-term results, at best. Well that's what you'll do here. Simply ignore him, be less available, plan activities with other people not including him, etc.

This way you're communicating without words that you're ready to walk away when he doesn't behave well and doesn't respect you. This is the best and proven way to get respect from a guy.

Don't ever bluff.

When he keeps treating you without respect, or when he's not behaving the way he should, walk away. Never bluff about leaving him.

I find it important to never get mad at him and say things like, "Well if you _____, then I'm gone." But if you ever do say something like that, then make sure you're actually gone if his behavior doesn't change right away.

If you bluff, you've just told him you don't respect yourself enough to follow up on it, and this will open the gates of disrespect. He simply won't care anymore since you've just shown him he can get away with almost anything.

Don't bluff, it's never a good strategy.

Don't nag.

Many women nag. I'm sure *you* would never nag; I'm talking to all the other women out there. I don't know why those women use it as a weapon, as a tool to hopefully change their man. As a relationship coach, I've studied hundreds of relationships and I've never found a healthy relationship where the woman nags and gets away with it. Ever.

Nagging will, at best, give short-term results; he'll do what you want to avoid a fight, or a negative atmosphere, but he won't be intrinsically motivated to take it to the next level. Men commit a lot easier when they thought it was *their* idea to take the next step. The other strategies in this book will make it easier for him to take that step.

One strategy to get what you want without nagging is to play with the attention and importance you accord to him (e.g., how available you are, how much time you free up to spend with him, etc.) Decrease that level if you want him to chase you harder; increase that level if you want him to feel at ease. Increase the level of importance even further if you want to raise his fear of commitment and eventually scare him away.

Give him the gift of missing you.

Never let him assume you're available whenever he calls to ask you out. If you're already in a relationship with him, make sure you plan plenty of activities with other people that do not include him. He needs to be able to miss you.

It's not when he's with you that he'll feel how important you are to him. It's when you're not around that he can feel the void you've left. Men need this; every type of man needs this.

A Normal Relationship Script for a Man

Normal men will follow a standard script when courting or in a relationship with you. This is another way to filter out game players: they won't follow the script.

When a man falls for you, he's going to court you. You always need to remember men want to fight for whatever it is they want; they want to earn it. They don't want to get it without effort. I never suggest you play hard to get, but this is the reason why playing hard to get will always deliver better results than giving yourself too soon and being all over a man and confessing your love for him too soon.

So in the early stages, he will put in a lot of effort to get you. He'll ask you out, contact you, talk to you, ask you how you are, pay for dinner, take you places, share important moments with you, and so on. Game players will do this as well. That said, the real player will go overboard and really flaunt all of their traits in order to seduce you.

It's the next phase, the one-month mark into the relationship, which reveals the first difference between the normal men and the game players. A normal guy will continue to put in an effort. Some men might actually increase their efforts. The more he falls in love with you, the more he'll try not to lose you.

Some men can go through a fear of commitment stage, but in general, they'll overcome this on their own if you don't start to push them or ask them where the relationship is going.

For a man, time is a precious asset. It can be spent working or building a (side) business; he can work out; he can use it to watch sports, or he can use it to hang out with friends. There are so many things men love to do that give them loads of pleasure and are NOT related to women. Contrary to popular belief, most normal men don't think about women and sex every six seconds.

Therefore, if he spends time with you, he values you. There are many other things he could be doing with his time, things he'd love to do, but he still decides to spend that time with you. That's one of the reasons why it's so important to never nag or ask a man to spend more time with you. Let him decide. That way you'll be able to gauge his real interest level in you.

I always say you should never listen to his words and always watch his actions. This is a great example of how you can gauge his actions to determine his true interest level.

Game players will spend as little time as possible with you, in order to still get what they want. If you nag, a game player might spend more time with you, but he's wearing his mask; he doesn't really want to be there, he just does it in order to not lose having sex with you or whatever the reasons are he's with you. Pretty cruel, I know. But I want you to know the truth.

Herein lies a problem. Some women find this challenging. This is exactly what attracts them to game players. They love the little bit of attention they can get from him; it makes them feel important. Please don't fall into this trap.

If you really need to put in an effort yourself to get some attention from the guy you're with, something's seriously wrong.

When to Let Him Go

If by now you've figured out that your man is actually playing games with you. When do you then decide it's time to move on?

Right away!

Life is too short to waste on the wrong kind of man, especially since he won't ever change. Either you accept him for who he is and how he treats you, or you decide to move on. To my clients, my advice is to immediately walk away when they discover they're involved with a player who sees no future for their relationship.

You'll need to start meeting new guys, and you won't be able to do that when you're still involved with him.

One of my clients is a great woman; she's sweet, good-looking, and fun with very charismatic eyes. She's a real catch, but when she became a client, she was dating a male model. A super handsome and tall guy who could almost get any woman he wanted. It took some digging from my part to figure out what type of man he was, since there were no signs he was cheating on her or even flirting with other women.

They had been in a relationship for more than a year; the relationship had hit a plateau. My client, let's call her Sarah, was ready to move in with him and get to the next phase of the relationship. He wasn't. He wanted to keep things just the way they were, but promised her they would eventually move in together at some point in the future.

Was he playing games with her?

I suspected he was. He got so much attention from other women that he couldn't live with the idea of being pinned down by Sarah. She was gorgeous, but I guessed he wanted to keep his options open. In my opinion, he was still waiting for a better woman, even though Sarah was a total catch.

I helped Sarah make up her mind by having the following conversation with her:

"Given that you cannot change a man, do you still want to be in this exact situation five years from now?"

"No", she replied. "I want to start thinking about having a family; I'm almost thirty, and I want to get to the next level."

I then told her, "Just imagine you're supposed to drive from Los Angeles to Miami, East to West. When you start your drive, you notice on the car compass that you're driving North. Four hours later, you're still driving North. You turn on your GPS, and you notice you're actually driving away from Miami—your destination. What would you do? Would you continue to drive North, hoping that you'll eventually arrive in Miami that way?"

"No way", she replied. "I'd take the next exit and find a better route to get to Miami—one that actually gets me there."

"Then you have your answer, and you know what to do with your relationship," I replied.

This was a very hard decision for her, but she broke up with him about one week later. Within one month, her ex-boyfriend (let's call him John) got a new gorgeous girlfriend he could play games with. Sarah, on the other hand, needed more time. She went out on many dates and kept giving me feedback after every date.

"I keep thinking about my ex. None of the men I date come even close to John," she said.

"That's OK. If it were easy to find Mr. Right, I would be out of a job. Finding the right guy is like hiring the perfect candidate, or even playing the lottery. You'll need to play a lot to win. Just hang in there and keep meeting new men. There's no need to start a relationship with a guy who's less than John; we're looking for a better version of him."

It took her four months of "interviewing" other men when she finally found the right guy. A great guy, good-looking, sense of humor, who already had a daughter and seemed to be a great dad. Their own child is now on the way, and she recently told me she was happier than ever. Leaving John was the best decision she ever made.

When you're sure that you're not going in the right direction, it's time to let him go. When you've given it some time, one year for instance, and there's no significant proof that anything will change, it's time to leave. Men don't change. You will always get the guy you chose.

Please, if you only remember one thing from this book, let it be this: **Men don't change. You will always get the guy you chose.** If he doesn't live up to your expectations and you don't want to settle for less (I suggest you don't), move on and start meeting other men.

One word of caution though. Men love a challenge. The moment you dump him, you might get some spastic reactions like, "Oh no, I don't want to lose you. Tell me what you want, I can change."

Don't listen to this. Please don't fall into this trap. He might not be playing a game when he pleads and tells you this, but men don't change. It's just his ego talking. Eventually, a couple of months later, you'll be in the exact same situation. Life is too short for that. Don't keep driving in the same direction if you know your final destination is in the opposite direction.

You Deserve a Great Guy, So Act Like It!

I've never met you, but I know you're a great person....I mean, you're still reading this book, right?

During my personal coaching sessions, I see so many fantastic women accept the disrespect by the man in their lives. It got me to dig a bit deeper. I wanted to find out why they allowed this behavior and why they thought it was OK.

It turned out that most of these amazing women didn't think they were anything special. They could have a lot of self-esteem and confidence in every area of their lives, but when it came to their guy, they always felt like he could walk away any second. Deep down, they thought they didn't deserve him.

Do you ever feel like this? Are you wondering if the dream can end any second? This wouldn't be weird. You're not alone.

A lot of women fear their great guy will leave them because he'll get tired of them or find someone new. This creates a self-fulfilling prophecy. They will act more needy, uptight, and jealous; they will not be the strong and emotionally stable women men desire.

You might not suffer from this particular fear, but it is crucial that you realize you deserve a great guy and act like it. If and when you do, everything in your love life will start to change. You'll become more of a challenge (men need this); you won't accept his bad behavior; you won't feel the need to get mad or uptight. You'll be able to walk away and create some space between the both of you and so on.

How important do you think you are? How important are you to yourself?

A man can never find you more important than you find yourself. Think about it. Sarah may be in a relationship with John, and John has adored her from the second they met. But if Sarah thinks John is out of her league, she'll start to make mistakes and John will eventually lower his interest level in her. This will happen on a subconscious level.

Did you ever see a below average woman in a healthy relationship with a great guy, where you though "wow, how did she get *him*"? Do you know what her secret is? She knows she's a catch, has a great personality, and is ready to walk away should she ever be treated badly.

Life is too short to not think you're great. Life is too short to accept disrespect from a guy. You always deserve better than that, and most importantly, you can always get better than that.

Most game players look for women they can prey upon. When a lion wants to have a gazelle for dinner, he's not going to run after the strongest and most secure gazelle; instead, he'll chase the weaker ones, especially ones that have been hurt before and are easy to capture.

Game players are no different. They look for women they can easily impress with their fancy words and compliments. They'll make you feel whole again, loved, and special.

When you've just met a guy, you may think, "Wow! This feels too good to be true. I hope I don't wake up and realize I was dreaming." Then let your alarm bells go off and objectively analyze the situation. You might be dealing with a game player. Sure, love is supposed to be great and should feel amazing, like a dream. But reality soon teaches us that when something seems to be too good to be true, it often is.

Just think of my earlier story. A great, successful guy proposes to a fantastic after only a couple of months of dating. Only a couple of weeks later, he broke up with her. He had had his fun. And the woman was left even weaker than she was before their relationship. After all of the personal problems she had faced lately, she had just been looking for a great guy to share the rest of her life with. Her vulnerability was emitting beams that this player's radar easily sensed. He knew exactly what to say and do to make her feel ecstatic. Beware of this kind of man.

You might be a super strong woman and think, "Brian, I would never let that happen. I'm too smart to be taken advantage of like that." This may be true, but everyone has phases in life where we feel down, vulnerable, and just need some love and attention. Game players will sense this and attack.

Final Thoughts

You've now learned who the game players are, why they do what they do, how you can spot them, and what you can do about it.

If you came to the conclusion that the man you're currently with might be playing games, then I wish you a lot of good luck. I know it's not easy at all to discover that someone you love might not be who he says he is. I hope this book taught you that you deserve better than a guy who's not honest with you.

You'll hopefully make the little tweaks I've mentioned and install the abundance mindset. There are plenty of great men out there—men who will treat you with the respect you deserve.

I want to thank you for reading. I had a blast writing this book and hope you'll find it helpful. I know there are 101 other things you could have done with your time, and I appreciate you spending it by reading this book.

I know I touch some tricky subjects, but I've tried to give you the hard and real truth about how men think, so you can benefit from it and finally understand my sometimes confusing gender.

If you've found this book helpful, then you'll love my other books:

F*CK Him: Nice Girls Always Finish Last

21 Traps You Need to Avoid in Dating and Relationships

Are You Scaring Him Away

Failure to launch: how to handle your commitment-phobic man

And if you want even more tips and strategies, sign up for my FREE advanced tactics newsletter on **RedFlagsBook.com** and join the now 23,653 women who already receive it. You'll get even more tips and techniques to better understand men. Some of them are:

- 2 ways to get a man to commit
- A little known strategy to get a guy to notice you
- How to find out if he really likes you

And much much more.

So come on over to **RedFlagsBook.com** and get the Free Tips.